LET'S INVESTIGATE
Number Patterns

LET'S INVESTIGATE
Number
Patterns

By Marion Smoothey

Illustrated by Ted Evans

MARSHALL CAVENDISH
NEW YORK · LONDON · TORONTO · SYDNEY

Library Edition Published 1993

© Marshall Cavendish Corporation 1993

Published by Marshall Cavendish Corporation
2415 Jerusalem Avenue
PO Box 587
North Bellmore
New York 11710

Series created by Graham Beehag Book Design

Library of Congress Cataloging-in-Publication Data

Smoothey, Marion, 1943-
    Number Patterns by Marion Smoothey; illustrated by Ted Evans.
        p. cm.. -- (Let's Investigate)
    Includes index.
    Summary: Introduces simple math concepts through a variety of
    problems and games.
    ISBN 1-85435-458-2   ISBN 1-85435-455-8 (set)
    1. Mathematics -- Juvenile literature. [1. Mathematics.
    2. Mathematical recreations.] I. Evans, Ted ill. II. Title. III. Series:
    Smoothey, Marion, 1943-   Let's Investigate.
    QA40.5.S56 1992   92-4629
    510---dc20   CIP
                                                            AC

Printed in Singapore by Times Offset PTE Ltd
Bound in the United States

Contents

Dots and Patterns

1. Michael Jackson
2. Charlie Chaplin
3. Winston Churchill
4. George Bush
5. Queen Elizabeth
6. Madonna

How many dots are there here?

What's in a Name?

In ancient times it was believed that a person had a magic number. The number was worked out by using a code for the letters of the person's name. If we use the code A = 1, B = 2, C = 3 and so on, the magic number for Batman is:

$$2 + 1 + 20 + 13 + 1 + 14 = 51.$$

B A T M A N

● Crack the code used here so that you can match the faces to the numbers.

1. 248

2. 238

3. 416

4. 214

5. 300

6. 124

◇ What is your magic number using this code?
◇ Do any of your friends have the same number as you?

Rectangular Numbers

There were 36 dots on page 7. Were you right?

If we arrange the 36 dots like this, we can count them much faster.

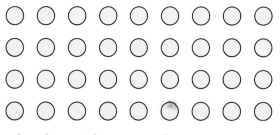

They make the shape of a rectangle.

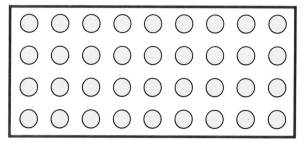

● How many other ways can 36 dots be arranged to make a rectangle?

Patterns with odd numbers

1st odd number = 1
2nd odd number = 3 = $(2 \times 2) - 1$
3rd odd number = 5 = $(3 \times 2) - 1$
4th odd number = 7 = $(? \times 2) - 1$
5th odd number = ? = $(? \times 2) - 1$

● 50th odd number = ?

Magic Squares

According to Chinese tradition, over four thousand years ago the Emperor Yu was standing on the banks of the Yellow River when he saw a tortoise. On its back was a magic square of numbers. The square was magic because, no matter which way the Emperor added up its lines, the numbers came to the same total.

Mathematicians in other countries found these magic squares fascinating too. Sometimes people wore them, engraved in gold or silver, as good luck charms.

● Some magic squares for you to copy and complete. Remember that the horizontal, vertical, and diagonal lines must each total the same number.

10

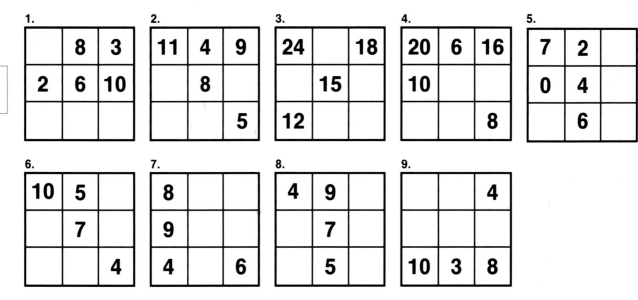

1.

	8	3
2	6	10

2.

11	4	9
	8	
		5

3.

24		18
	15	
12		

4.

20	6	16
10		
		8

5.

7	2	
0	4	
	6	

6.

10	5	
	7	
		4

7.

8		
9		
4		6

8.

4	9	
	7	
	5	

9.

		4
10	3	8

● What do you notice about the last four squares?

Investigation

Look again at Emperor Yu's magic square on page 9.

● What is the magic number which all the lines total?

● What is the total of all the numbers?

Answer the same two questions for the other magic squares which you completed. Record your answers in a table like the one on page 12

Keep your answers. You will need them.

Other ways of making rectangles with 36 dots

Which arrangement is the easiest to count?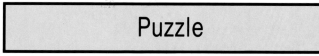

Perhaps you found 6 rows of 6 the quickest. This makes the shape of a special rectangle – a square.

● Arrange these numbers as rectangular arrangements of dots. Find as many different arrangements as you can for each number: 9, 12, 16, 24, 32 and 49.

Puzzle

● If a rectangular number always has a pattern of at least two rows and two columns, are there any numbers, other than 1, which are not rectangular?

Check your results for the magic squares.

Question	Magic Number	Total of all the numbers
Emporer Yu's square	15	45
1	18	54
2	24	72
3	45	135
4	42	126
5	12	36
6	21	63
7	21	63
8	21	63
9	21	63

- What is the connection between the magic number and the total of all the numbers?

- Write out the numbers of Emperor Yu's square in ascending order.

4	3	8
9	5	1
2	7	6

- What is the middle number?

- What are the connections between the middle number, the magic number and the total of all the numbers?

Study your list of the numbers and compare it with the way they are arranged in the square.

- Which is the middle number in your list and in the square?

- What pairs of numbers each side of the middle one are there in the list and in the square?

If you're stuck, page 15 might help.

Making your own magic squares

● Use the counting numbers from 2 to 10 to make a magic square.

● Use the even numbers from 2 to 18 to make a magic square.

Investigations

● **1.** Investigate using your own groups of numbers to make a magic square. Can you find any rules to help you decide whether or not a group of numbers will make a magic square?

● **2.** Investigate different sized magic squares. What rules can you find?

More magic squares to copy and complete.

1.

		1	14
2		8	
			5
9	6	15	4

2.

16	2		13
5		10	
9	7		12
4			1

3.

	8		1
3	10		15
2		7	14
	5		4

4.

21		8	18
10		15	
	12	11	
9			6

Answers to page 11

14

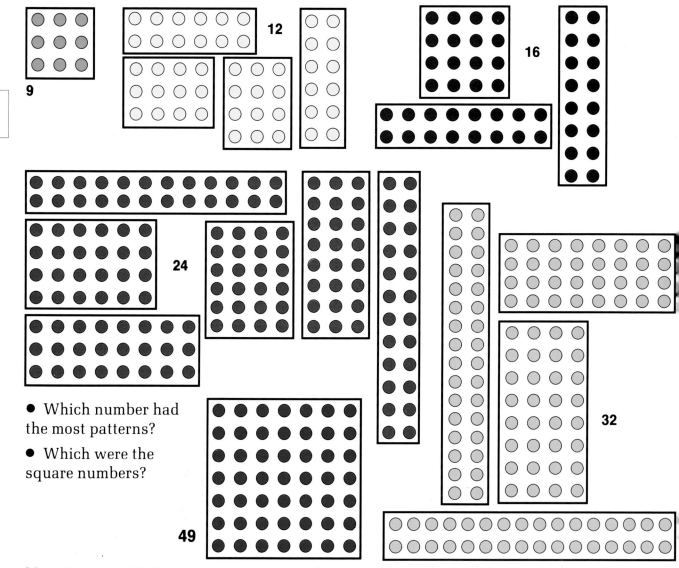

● Which number had the most patterns?

● Which were the square numbers?

Numbers which are not rectangular

Prime numbers, such as 2, 3, 5, 7, 11, 13 and 17, are not rectangular. This is because they can only be divided exactly by themselves and 1.

● Find the first five square numbers – 1 is the first.

Turn to page 16.

Help with magic squares

The total of all the numbers is
always 3 times the magic number.

Total of all numbers = 45
Total of each line = 15 (the magic number)
45 = 3 × 15

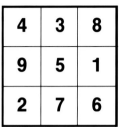

The magic number is always 3
times the middle number.

Total of all lines = 15 (the magic number)
The middle number = 5
15 = 3 × 5

The total of all the numbers is
always 9 times the middle number.

Total of all numbers = 45
The middle number = 5
45 = 9 × 5

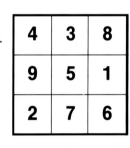

The middle number in the list
below is also the middle number of
the square.

1 2 3 4 |5| 6 7 8 9

Pairs of numbers in the list below
match pairs of numbers in the
square.

1 2 3 4 |5| 6 7 8 9

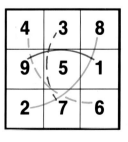

Try the investigations on page 13.

Square Numbers

Answers to page 14

16

The first five square numbers are: 1, 4, 9, 16, and 25.

Investigation

Look at some of the patterns which can be built up from the first five square numbers.

1st square   1
2nd square $4 = 1 + 3$ (sum of first two odd numbers) $= 1^2 + 3$
(1^2 means 1×1 or 1 squared)
3rd square $9 = 1 + 3 + 5$ (sum of first three odd numbers) $= 4 + 5$ $= 2^2 + 5$
4th square $16 = 1 + 3 + 5 + 7$ (sum of first four odd numbers) $= 9 + 7$ $= 3^2 + 7$
5th square $25 = 1 + 3 + 5 + 7 + 9$ (sum of first five odd numbers) $= 16 + 9$ $= 4^2 + 9$

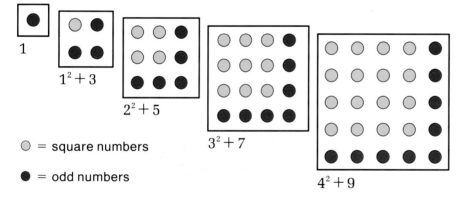

$\bigcirc$ = square numbers

$\bullet$ = odd numbers

- Find the next three square numbers, by continuing the patterns.

- How can you use a square number to find the sum of the first 15 odd numbers?

- If you are told that $17^2 = 289$, how can you work out 18^2 without a calculator or long multiplication?

☆ **Hint: think about the patterns on page 8 and on this page.**

Triangular Numbers

At the start of a game of pool, 15 balls are arranged in a triangle.

You can think of the rows of balls in the frame as a series of triangles, getting bigger a row at a time.

1st triangle = 1 ball
2nd triangle = 3 balls = 1st triangle + 2
3rd triangle = 6 balls = 2nd triangle + 3
4th triangle = 10 balls = 3rd triangle + 4
5th triangle = 15 balls = 4th triangle + ?

● Continue the pattern to find the 7th triangle number. Check your answer by drawing.

If we join together the 5th and 6th triangles, the result is a square.

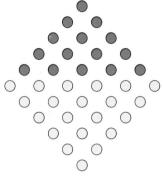

18

The 5th triangle number + the 6th triangle number = the 6th square number.

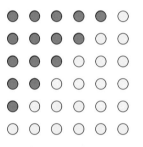

Half of the 6th square number is 3 less than the 6th triangle number.

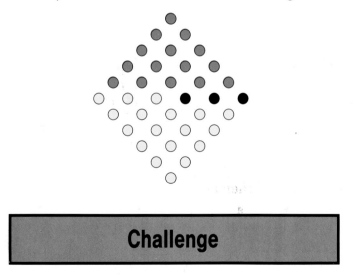

Challenge

Using what you know about square and triangular numbers, calculate the 10th triangular number.

The Number Cruncher

*The Number Cruncher is a mean machine.
A number goes in, a number comes out.
What goes on can't be seen.*

The Number Cruncher can be programmed to change numbers, according to a rule.

Here the rule is Add 4. We put in the counting numbers from 1 to 10. The numbers which come out are the counting numbers from 5 to 14.

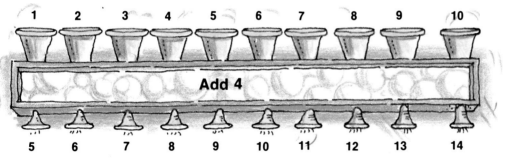

The Number Cruncher can do more than one thing to each number. Here the rule is "Multiply by 2 and then add 1."

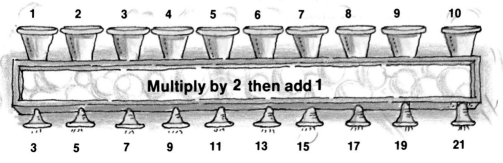

What has the Number Cruncher done to each number?
Remember that the rule must work for EVERY pair of numbers.

1.

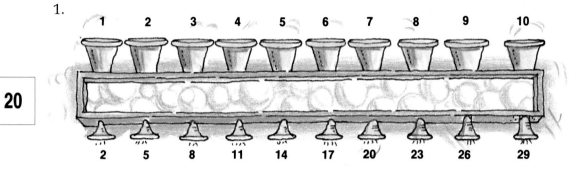

What are the rules for these?

2.

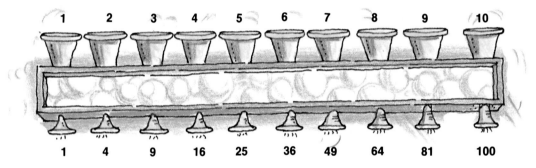

You've met some of these numbers before on page 16.

3.

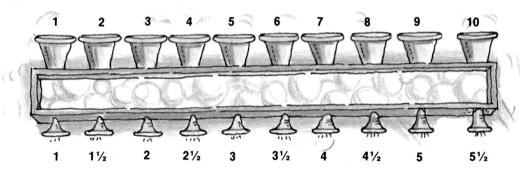

4.

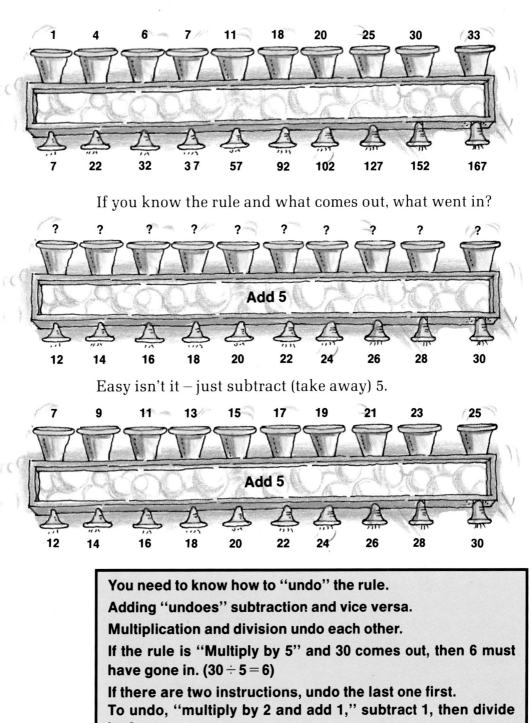

1	4	6	7	11	18	20	25	30	33
7	22	32	37	57	92	102	127	152	167

If you know the rule and what comes out, what went in?

?	?	?	?	?	?	?	?	?	?
Add 5									
12	14	16	18	20	22	24	26	28	30

Easy isn't it – just subtract (take away) 5.

7	9	11	13	15	17	19	21	23	25
Add 5									
12	14	16	18	20	22	24	26	28	30

You need to know how to "undo" the rule.

Adding "undoes" subtraction and vice versa.

Multiplication and division undo each other.

If the rule is "Multiply by 5" and 30 comes out, then 6 must have gone in. (30 ÷ 5 = 6)

If there are two instructions, undo the last one first.
To undo, "multiply by 2 and add 1," subtract 1, then divide by 2.

5.

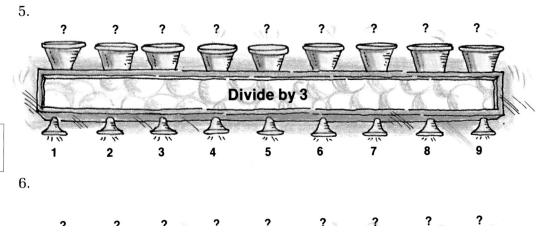

Divide by 3

1 2 3 4 5 6 7 8 9

6.

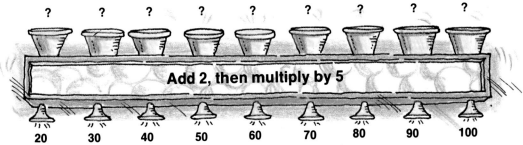

Add 2, then multiply by 5

20 30 40 50 60 70 80 90 100

7.

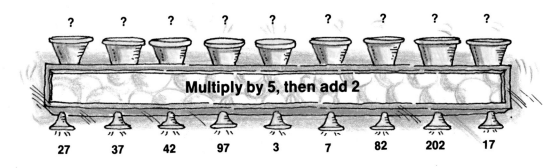

Multiply by 5, then add 2

27 37 42 97 3 7 82 202 17

A Card Trick

How to work out the trick for the ace of spades

$1 \times 2 = 2$
$2 + 1 = 3$
$3 \times 5 = 15$

Add on 4 for a spade
$15 + 4 = 19$

Working back, $19 - 4 = 15$ must be a spade

$15 \div 5 = 3$
$3 - 1 = 2$
$2 \div 2 = 1$

The card is the ace of spades!

You need to practice first.

Count the Jacks as 11, the Queens as 12 and the Kings as 13.

Take a card from a pack of playing cards. Look at the number.

Double the number of the card, and then add 1. Then multiply the result by 5.

If the card is a club add on 1, if a heart add on 2, if its a diamond add on 3 and add on 4 if its a spade.

By working back from the total and "undoing" the instructions, you can say which card was chosen. Your first step is to take off 1, 2, 3 or 4 to get a number which you can divide exactly by 5.

When you have memorized the instructions and made sure you can get the right answer, ask a friend to choose a card without showing it to you. Tell her what calculations to perform, and then you can amaze her by knowing what card she picked!

If you think these numbers make it too easy to see how the trick is done, experiment with instructions of your own. Check with several cards to make sure they always work.

Very Large and Very Small Numbers

24

When we write a number, the position of the numerals is important.

19 is not the same as 91. 19 is 1 ten and 9 ones. 91 is 9 tens and 1 one.

Zero is also very important. If we write 91,000 we mean 91 thousand, not 91. The zero is useful for writing large and small numbers. For example, 0.001″ is one thousandth of an inch.

Sometimes, people need to use such large or small numbers that it would take far too long to write all the necessary zeros.

Engineers measure in microns, with a micrometer, when they cut metal on a lathe. A micron is one millionth of a meter. The diameter of a human hair is 5 microns. But scientists and astronomers need to use even smaller numbers, and some so huge that we cannot really imagine them.

The mass of an electron in an atom is
0.000 000 000 000 000 000 000 000 000 9 grams.

The mass of the sun is
1,991,200,000,000,000,000,000,000,000 kilograms.

The largest number which has a name is the centrillion.
This is 1 followed by 600 zeros!

25

All these zeros can be very confusing and take a long time to write. There is a shorter way of writing them. It uses the patterns of ten in our number system.

tens of thousands	thousands	hundreds	tens	units	tenths	hundredths
10,000	1,000	100	10	1	0.1	0.01
$10 \times 10 \times 10 \times 10$	$10 \times 10 \times 10$	10×10	10×1	1	$\frac{1}{10}$	$\frac{1}{10 \times 10}$

You can write the second row of the pattern in a shorter way.

10,000	1,000	100	10	1	0.1	0.01
10^4	10^3	10^2			10^{-1}	10^{-2}

The small number above the 10 is called the **power** or the **index**. It tells you how many times 10 has been multiplied or divided by itself. The negative numbers mean divide.

Fill in the missing parts of the pattern.

This pattern can help us to write any number.

We use the number of times a number is multiplied, or divided by 10, to write it in **scientific notation**.

30,000	6,000	0.007
$3 \times 10,000$	$6 \times 1,000$	7×0.001
3×10^4	6×10^3	7×10^{-3}

30,854	6,122	0.00753
3.0854×10^4	6.122×10^3	7.53×10^{-3}

In scientific notation the first number has to be greater than 1, and less than 10. The power of 10 tells you how many places the decimal point has been moved to change the number to scientific notation.

● Try writing these numbers in scientific notation.

13,000   **710 million**   **0.00004**

0.000781   **a centrillion**

Powers can be used with any number; not only 10. 3^4 means $3 \times 3 \times 3 \times 3$ which equals 81.

A story, which probably originated in India, shows how quickly numbers can increase using powers. According to legend, the game of chess was invented in India. The emperor was so pleased with its inventor that he invited him to name his own reward.

The inventor made what seemed a modest request for a grain of rice on the first square of the chess board, two grains on the second, four on the third, eight on the fourth and so on.

We can write the inventor's clever request by using powers:

grains on 1st square $1 = 2^0$
grains on 2nd square $2 = 2^1$
grains on 3rd square $4 = 2^2 \ (2 \times 2)$
grains on 4th square $8 = 2^3 \ (2 \times 2 \times 2)$

grains on 20th square $? = 2^?$
grains on 64th square $9.2234 \times 10^{18} = 2^{63}$
(using a pocket calculator)

To find the total amount of rice, you now need to add together the grains on each square.

Look at the patterns and find an easy way of doing this.

Number of square	Number of grains on square	Sum of grains	Pattern
1	$2^0 = 1$	1	$2^1 - 1$
2	$2^1 = 2$	3	$2^2 - 1$
3	$2^2 = 4$	7	$2^3 - 1$
4	$2^3 = 8$	15	$2^4 - 1$
5	$2^4 = 16$	31	$? - 1$
6	$2^5 = ?$	?	$? - 1$
64	$2^? = ?$	?	$2^? - 1$

You need a calculator with a power function button (y^x) to figure this out. The calculator's display will not have the room to show you all the digits, but it will tell you the size of the number in scientific notation.

● To get an idea of what a huge number this really is, try to figure out how many trucks the inventor would need to transport his rice.

Weigh out a small amount of rice and count the grains. Assume you are using 40 ton trucks.

The Fibonacci Sequence

Investigation

What patterns can you see in these numbers?

1   1   2   3   5   8   1 3   2 1

● What would the next three numbers be?

This sequence was first investigated by an Italian mathematician, Leonardo of Pisa, in the thirteenth century. Because his nickname was Fibonacci, these numbers are often called the Fibonacci sequence.

Some suggestions to try.

1. Find the **difference** between each pair of numbers. What sequence appears?

2. Choose a series of four numbers from the sequence;
    3, 5, 8, 13.
multiply the first and last together;
    3×13
write down the number;
    39
multiply the middle two numbers together and record the result;
    $5 \times 8 = 40$
find the difference between the two numbers;
    $40 - 39 = 1$
Repeat this for other groups of four numbers. What happens?

3. Choose a series of three numbers;
    5, 8, 13
multiply the outside numbers;
    $5 \times 13 = 65$
and square the middle one
    $8^2 = 64$
What is the difference?
    $65 - 64 = ?$
Is it always the same no matter which group of three you choose?

4. Choose a series of three or more numbers;
    1, 1, 2, 3, 5
square all the numbers except the last and add the results;
    $1^2 + 1^2 + 2^2 + 3^2 = 1 + 1 + 4 + 9 = 15$
multiply the last and the next to last numbers together;
    $3 \times 5 = 15$
Note the result. They are the same answers.

● Does it always happen for any group you choose?

5. Write down the sequence up to 233.

Divide each number by the one before it and record the result.

    $1 \div 1 = 1$
    $2 \div 1 = 2$
    $3 \div 2 = 1.5$
    $5 \div 3 = 1.67$
    $8 \div 5 = ?$
    $? \div 8 = ?$

● What happens?

30

The ruins of the Parthenon still remain in Athens. It was built in the fifth century B.C.

Measure the sides of the rectangle enclosing the Parthenon. Divide the long side by the short side.

● Where have you seen these numbers before?

The Fibonacci sequence turns up in the strangest places. If you get the chance, count the bumps on a pineapple! Mark a bump on the base and count how many there are up to the stalk in the clockwise spiral and the counter-clockwise spiral.

You might also try looking at the patterns in the spirals of the yellow center of a daisy and of a pine cone.

Investigating Dots and Lines

32

Draw three dots, not in a line.

•

•

•

Draw as many straight lines as possible, with a dot at each end.

Make a table to record your results.

Dots	Lines
3	3

Repeat the instructions for 4 dots, 5 dots, 6 dots and so on.

- How many lines could you draw to join 101 dots?
- Where have you seen this pattern before?

Investigating Number Chains

Think of a number.
50
If it is even, halve it.
50 ⇨ **25**
If it is odd, add 1.
50 ⇨ **25** ⇨ **26**
Continue.
100 ⇨ **50** ⇨ **25** ⇨ **26** ⇨ **13** ⇨ **. . .**

● **1.** Try starting with several different numbers. What happens?

◇ Investigate changing the rules.

● **2.** What happens if you add 3 to the odd numbers?

● **3.** Try dividing the "evens" by 4 istead of by 2.

◇ Can you tell which rules will work and which will not?

Elevenses

Sometimes we need to be careful about looking for patterns. A calculator with a power function (y^x) will help you to build up this pattern. But you can easily do it by multiplying as well.

$$11^1 = 11 \times 1 = 11$$
$$11^2 = 11 \times 11 = 121$$
$$11^3 = 121 \times 11 = 1,331$$
$$11^4 = 1,331 \times 11 = 14,641$$

● How is the pattern building up? Do you think it will continue?

◇ Write down what you think 11^5 is, without using a calculator or multiplying.

◇ Check to see if you were right.

Number Games For Two

You need a piece of paper and two different colored pencils.

Write down the numbers from 1 to 9 on the paper.

Take turns crossing out one of the numbers.

Use one color for each person.

The object of the game is to be first to make a total of 15 with any three of the numbers you have crossed out. You may only cross out each number once.

Move 1

Red's move   2 3 4 5 6 7 8 9

                              4

Move 2

Black's move   1 2 3 4 5 6 7 8 9

                              6

Move 3

Red's move   1 2 3 4 5 6 7 8 9

                        4 + 9

Move 4

Black's move   1 2 3 4 5 6 7 8 9

             6 + 2   **Why choose 2?**

Move 5

Red's move   1 2 3 4 5 6 7 8 9

             4 + 9 + 7   **Why choose 7?**

Move 6

Black's move   1 2 3 4 5 6 7 8 9

             6 + 2 + 8   **Black is in a winning position now**

Move 7

Red's move 2 3 4 5 6 7 8 9

4 + 9 + 7 + 5   Red tries to stop black (8 + 2 + 5 = 15)

Move 8

Black's move 1 2 3 4 5 6 7 8 9

6 + 2 + 8 + 1   Black still wins

35

A variation is to draw a double cross. One player takes the odd numbers from 1 to 9, and the other takes the even numbers from 2 to 8. The player with the odd numbers starts. You can only use each number once.

The winner is the first one to complete a line of any three numbers (odd or even) which total 15.

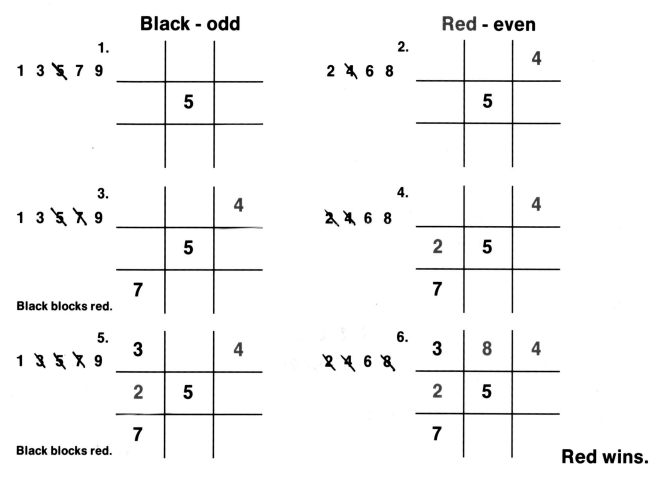

Black - odd   **Red - even**

1.   2.
1 3 5 7 9   2 4 6 8

Black blocks red.

5.   6.
1 3 5 7 9   2 4 6 8

Black blocks red.   **Red wins.**

Black - odd   **Red - even**

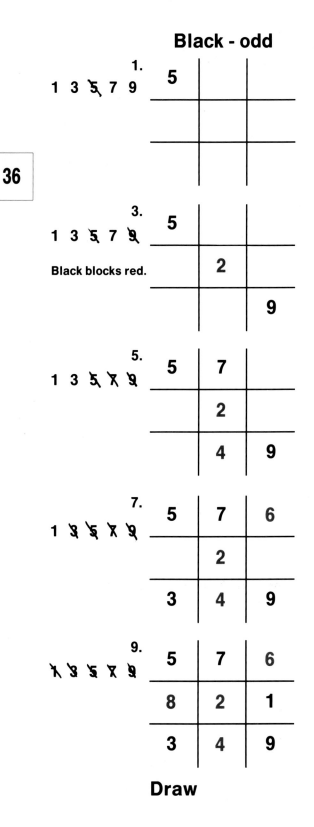

1.
1 3 5̶ 7 9   5 | |

2.
2̶ 4 6 8   5 | |
| | 2 |

36

3.
1 3 5̶ 7 9̶   5 | |
Black blocks red. | 2 |
| | 9

4.
2̶ 4̶ 6 8   5 | |
| | 2 |
| 4 | 9

5.
1 3 5̶ 7̶ 9̶   5 | 7 |
| 2 |
| 4 | 9

6.
2̶ 4̶ 6̶ 8   5 | 7 | 6
Red blocks black. | 2 |
| 4 | 9

7.
1 3̶ 5̶ 7̶ 9̶   5 | 7 | 6
| 2 |
3 | 4 | 9

8.
2̶ 4̶ 6̶ 8̶   5 | 7 | 6
| 8 | 2 |
3 | 4 | 9

9.
1̶ 3̶ 5̶ 7̶ 9̶   5 | 7 | 6
8 | 2 | 1
3 | 4 | 9

Draw

◇ If you investigated magic squares, you should be able to think of some strategies which might help to win these games.

◇ Is there an advantage in being the first player? Is there a best number to begin with? Do the same things work for both games?

Three Quick Puzzles

Numbers around a triangle

● How many ways can you arrange the numbers 1 to 6 around a triangle so that the total of each side is the same?

● How can you be sure that you have found all the ways?

These numbers are incorrect. Try your own solutions, there are various ways in which you can get the same numbers on each side.

```
                    1
                    ●
   6      2              6      12
          ●              ●
       3       4      5
       ●       ●      ●
             12
```

Numbers from 1 to 10

● Using the numbers 1, 2, 3 and 4, and any mathematical signs you like, such as $+$, $-$, $\times$, $\div$, ( ), make the numbers from 1 to 10. You must use all 4 numbers once each time.

To get you started; a way of making 1 is $(3 \div 1) - (4 \div 2)$. Now you find another.

Star number

● Arrange the numbers from 1 to 7 so that each row of the star totals the same.

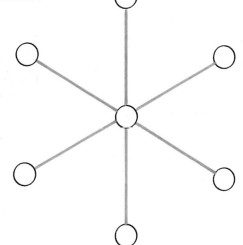

Heads and Tails

If you toss a coin, it can land heads or tails.
If you toss 2 coins together, there are 4 ways in which they can land.

HH   HT   TH   TT

How many ways can 3 coins land?

HHH	HTH	THT	TTT
	HHT	TTH	
	THH	HTT	

We can arrange these results in a pattern.

1 coin, total 2.

    H   T
    (1)   (1)

2 coins, total 4.

  H H   H T T H   T T
  (1)   (2)   (1)

3 coins, total 8.

H H H	H T H	T H T	T T T
	H H T	T T H	(1)
	T H H	H T H	
	(3)	(3)	

● List the ways in which four coins could land. Try to arrange them to continue the pattern.

Routes Through a Maze

You have to work your way down the maze to one of the exits. At the entrance to the maze, you can either turn left or right. You have this choice at each junction. You are not allowed to go back up.

There are 2 routes to **a**. We can record them as LR (left, right) and RL (right, left).

There are 3 routes to **b**. LRR, RRL and

● List the routes to each of the exits. Record your results carefully.

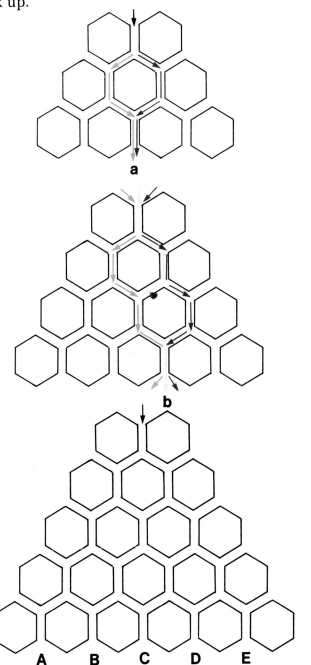

Patterns with coins

Your pattern for tossing four coins should look like this.

					TOTAL		
1 **H**		**1** **T**					
					2	1 coin	2^1 ways
1 **HH**	**2** **HT TH**	**1** **TT**					
					4	2 coins	2^2 ways
1 **HHH**	**3** **HTH** **HHT** **THH**		**3** **THT** **TTH** **HTT**	**1** **TTT**			
					8	3 coins	2^3 ways
1 **HHHH**	**4** **HHHT** **HHTH** **HTHH** **THHH**	**6** **HHTT** **TTHH** **HTHT** **THTH** **THHT** **HTTH**	**4** **TTTH** **TTHT** **THTT** **HTTT**	**1** **TTTT**			
					16	4 coins	2^4 ways

● You can use the pattern to predict how many ways 5 coins can fall.

Maze route patterns

A	LLLL	1 route	D	LRRR		
B	RLLL			RLRR		
	LRLL			RRLR		
	LLRL			RRRL	4 routes	
	LLLR	4 routes	E	RRRR	1 route	
C	LRLR					
	RLRL					
	LLRR					
	RRLL					
	RLLR					
	LRRL	6 routes				

● What do you notice about these two sets of results?

Pascal's Triangle

Blaise Pascal was born in France in 1623. He was a child prodigy, who was fascinated by mathematics. When Pascal was nineteen, he invented the first calculating machine which actually worked. This was something Fibonacci had tried to do before and had failed.

One of the topics which interested Pascal was the likelihood of an event occurring. His interest was triggered by a gambler. The gambler asked Pascal to help him make better guesses about which scores would be most likely when two dice were thrown.

In the course of his investigations, Pascal produced the triangular pattern of numbers which now bears his name. The pattern was known to the Chinese three hundred years before, but it was Pascal who developed it fully.

42

```
                        1
                     1     1
                  1     2     1
               1     3     3     1
            1     4     6     4     1
         1     5    10    10    5     1
      1     6    15    20    15    6     1
   1     7    21    35    35    21    7     1
1     8    28    56    70    56    28    8     1
1   9   36   84   126   126   84   36   9   1
1  10  45  120  210  252  210  120  45  10  1
```

● Study Pascal's triangle and see how many patterns you can find in it.

● The counting numbers are there. Where?

● Which row gives the same pattern as tossing four coins and the routes through the maze?

● Which row gives you the answer to predicting how many ways five coins can fall?

● You will notice that the "Elevenses" pattern on page 33 is found in the triangle, but only up to 11^4. After that you have to add digits in the triangle to make it work. It is not always wise to assume that a pattern continues!

$11^4 = 1\ 4\ 6\ 4\ 1$
5th row of Pascal's triangle $= 1\ 4\ 6\ 4\ 1$

$11^5 = 1\ 6\ 1\ 0\ 5\ 1$
6th row of Pascal's triangle $= 1\ 5\ 10\ 10\ 5\ 1$

If you add the digits and ignore the zeros in the triangle, you can make the numbers the same as 11^5. This works for 11^6 as well. Try it.

● Inside the triangle are small triangles, which help you to work out the next row.

● Can you find a row of triangular numbers?

● Total each row of numbers and write the answer as a power of 2. What will the total be for the 10th row?

$1 = 2^0$ 1st row
$2 = 2^1$ 2nd row
$4 = 2^2$ 3rd row
$8 = 2^3$ 4th row

```
              1
            1   1
          1 + 2   1
        1  \3/  3   1
      1   4   6   4   1
    1   5   10 \10 + 5/ 1
  1   6   15  20 \15/ 6   1
1 \7 + 21/ 35  35  21  7   1
  1  8 \28/ 56  70  56  28  8   1
1   9   36 84 126 126 84 36  9   1    10th row
```

● In these diagrams of the triangle, groups of numbers have been shaded. Identify the group and describe the pattern.

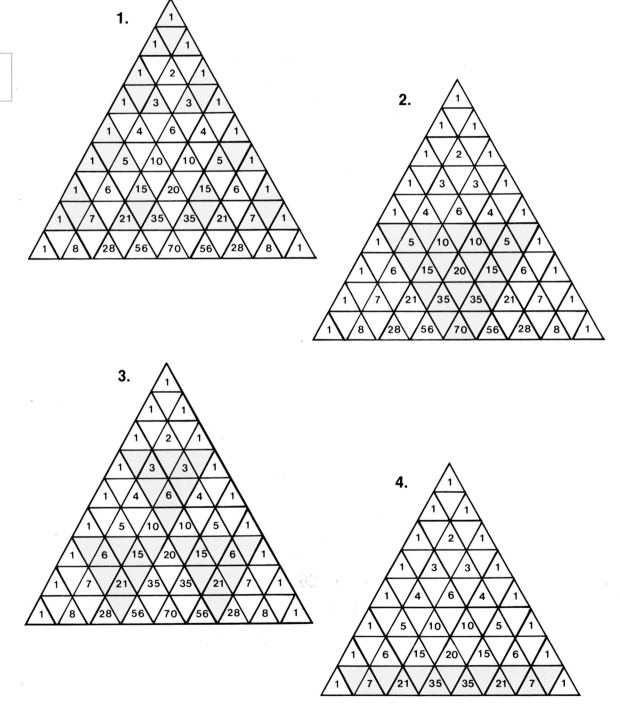

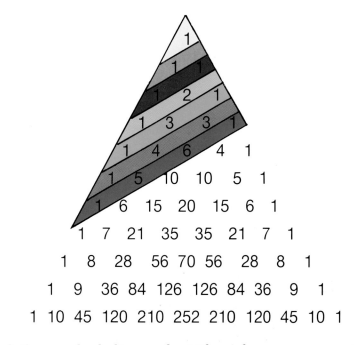

● Total the marked diagonals. Where have you seen these numbers

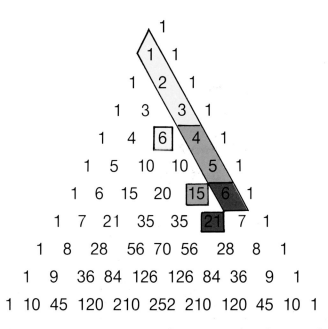

● Can you find the connection between the diagonal numbers and the numbers in the squares?

● What is the sum of $1 + 2 + 3 + 4 + 5 + 6 + 7 + 8 + 9$?

Paper Folding

Cut a long strip of paper.

Fold it in half once.

Record the result in a table like this.

Number of Times Folded	Number of Sections	Number of Creases

Repeat as many times as you can.

● Study the pattern in the table. If it were possible to fold the paper ten times, how many sections and how many creases would there be?

A Bee Family Tree

A drone, a male bee, has only one parent, a queen. A queen has two parents, a drone and a queen.

The family tree below traces the parent and grandparents of a drone. Continue the tree back for another three generations. Note the number of ancestors in each generation.

● Can you predict the number of ancestors seven generations back without drawing the tree?

● What is this sequence of numbers called?

Patterns in a Number Square

48

1. Look at the pattern of shading in the number square. What kind of numbers have been shaded? Will the squares lettered A, B, C and D be shaded?

2. Which numbers have been shaded this time? Will the lettered squares be shaded?

3. This is a harder one.

1.

1	2	3	4	5	6	7	8	9	10
11	12	13	14	15	16	17	18	19	20
21	22	23	24	25	26	27	28	29	30
31	32	33	34	35	36	37	38	39	40
41	42	43							
			A						
				B					
									C
			D						100

2.

1	2	3	4	5	6	7	8	9	10
11	12	13	14	15	16	17	18	19	20
21	22	23	24	25	26	27	28	29	
	A		B						
				C					
				D					
									100

3.

1	2	3	4	5	6	7	8	9	10
11	12	13	14	15	16	17	18	19	20
21	22	23	24	25	26	27	28	29	30
		A		B			C		
				D					100

4. This time the numbers are arranged differently. Look at the shaded pattern. What will be the numbers in the lettered squares? You should know without counting around.

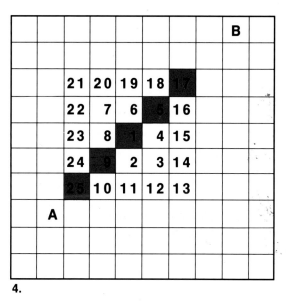

4.

In which square will the number 100 be?

5. This one is similar.

5.

● In these squares, there is one pattern in the horizontal numbers and another in the vertical ones. Use the patterns to work out the lettered squares.

50

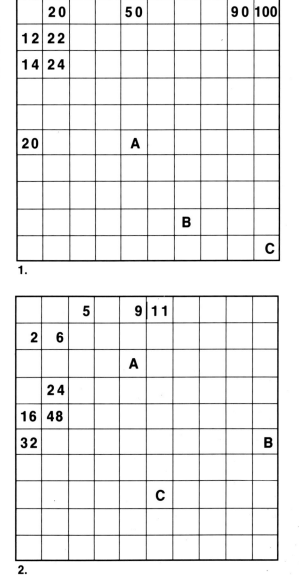

1.

2.

3.

◇ You can prepare similar squares for your friends to work out.

Windows

● This is a window looking into a number square from 1 to 100, like the first one on page 48. What kind of numbers have been shaded?

A pair, or a group, can play Windows Hangman.

The challenger prepares a window on a larger grid, shading in some multiples. In the large grid, all the numbers follow in sequence but they do not necessarily start at 1.

All that the other players see is the window and the shading, not the whole square and no numbers.

This gap of three spaces is a clue that the multiples of 4 have been shaded in the window.

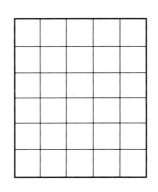

3	4	5	6	7	8	9	10	11
12	13						19	20
21	22						28	29
30	31						37	38
39	40						46	47
48	49						55	56
57	58	59	60	61	62	63	64	65

Each player takes a turn to guess a number which they think is in the window. If the guess is correct, the number is written in the window. If it is wrong, a part of the hangman is drawn.

If the window is completed before the man is hanged, the challenger has lost.

If you want to, you can specify the minimum size of window. The smaller the window, the harder it is to guess.

**First guess
number 1
(not in
the window)**

**Second guess
number 10
(not in
the window)**

**Third guess
number 15**

**Fourth and fifth
guesses,
numbers 16 and 17**

**Sixth guess
number 20
(next multiple of 4 after 16)
(not in the window)**

**Seventh guess
number 24
(next multiple of 4 after 20)**

	15	16	17	
	24			

**Eighth and ninth guesses,
numbers 25 and 26**

	15	16	17	
	24	25	26	

**Tenth guess
number 33
(adding down in nines)**

	15	16	17	
	24	25	26	
	33			

The players can now
complete the square – the
challenger has lost.

Investigating Frogs

The blue and the green frogs have to get back to their territories. The green frogs live on the island and the blue frogs live on the river bank.

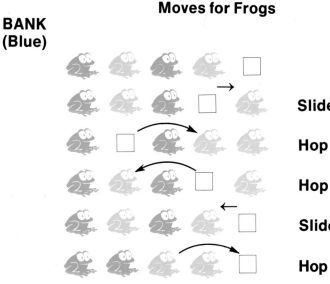

- Can you return them to their correct territory?

Frogs can slide or hop into a space, but only toward their own territory. They can only hop over a different colored frog.

Moves for Frogs

BANK (Blue)　　　　　　　　　　　　**ISLAND (Green)**

Slide

Hop

Hop not allowed – wrong direction

Slide not allowed – wrong direction

Hop not allowed over same color frog

It might help to represent them on a piece of paper, like this:

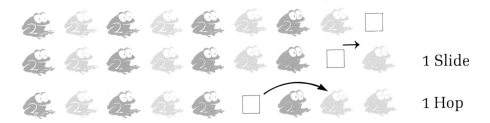

1 Slide

1 Hop

Alternatively, you can use colored counters, or colored pieces of paper.

● How many moves does it take to get all these frogs in the right place?

Sometimes it helps to solve a complicated problem if you begin with a simplified version.

Suppose we only have two frogs:

it takes 1 move, a slide, to get them home.

For three frogs:

it takes 2 moves, a hop and a slide.

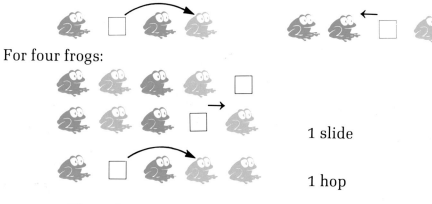

For four frogs:

	1 slide
	1 hop
	1 slide 3 moves

It begins to look as if it takes one less move than the number of frogs, but we had better do one more to make sure.

For five frogs:

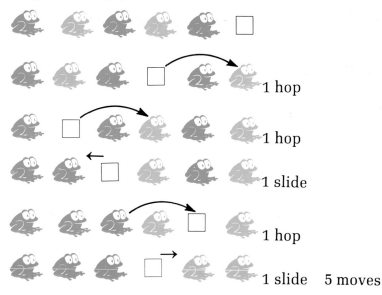

	1 hop
	1 hop
	1 slide
	1 hop
	1 slide 5 moves

Our theory has broken down!
Back to the drawing board! Work out how many moves are needed for six frogs.

☆ **Hint: if you get two frogs of the same color next to each other in the middle, you will get stuck. Keep a space between them.**

Another thing which often helps in investigations is to make a table of results to help to spot patterns.

This is the kind which might be useful here.

Number of frogs	Number of moves
2	1
3	2
4	3
5	5
6	

Complete the table up to 8 frogs. You may have already gotten the answer to 8 frogs from page 55.

Your completed table should look like this:

Number of Frogs	Number of moves
2	1
3	2
4	3
5	5
6	6
7	9
8	10

This doesn't look very helpful. There doesn't seem to be a pattern across the rows or down the columns. But if we rearrange the table into odd and even numbers of frogs, a pattern appears.

Even numbers of frogs	Number of moves	Odd numbers of frogs	Number of moves
1st even number (2)	1	2nd odd number (3)	2
2nd even number (4)	3	3rd odd number (5)	5
3rd even number (6)	6	4th odd number (7)	9
5th even number (8)	10		

Consider the pattern of the even numbers: 1, 3, 6, 10. It's the triangular numbers again. How many moves will 10 frogs take?

Now look at the odd numbers in the table. Compare each odd number with the next even number. How many moves will 9 frogs take?

You can go further and investigate what happens if the blank space is not at the end of the row.

This can make a good game to get a party going. Sit boys and girls, instead of blue and green frogs, on a row of chairs with a spare chair at the end. Ask volunteers to move all the girls to one end and all the boys to the other, using the rules for frogs.

If you haven't seen this puzzle before and learned the strategies, it is quite hard to do and everybody soon wants to have a try.

Calendar Patterns

Look at the calendar for August 1991.

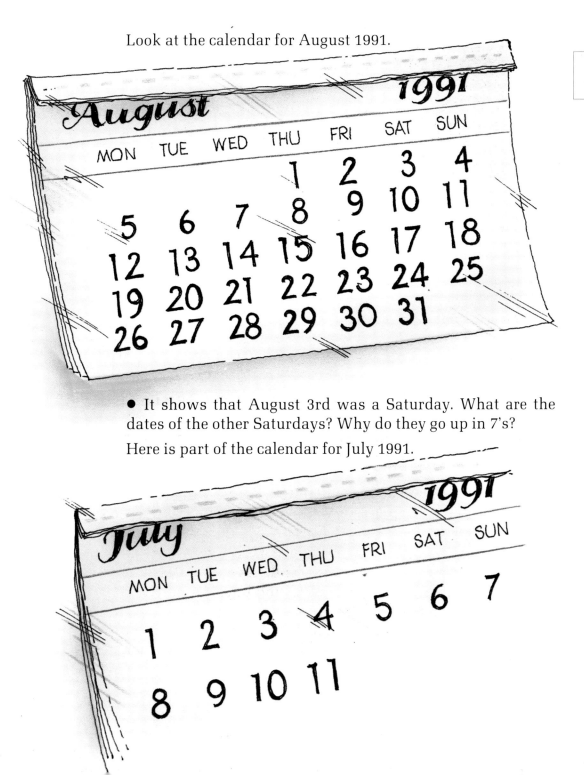

● It shows that August 3rd was a Saturday. What are the dates of the other Saturdays? Why do they go up in 7's?

Here is part of the calendar for July 1991.

● What was the date of the last Monday of July 1991? What day was the 24th? This rhyme will help you.

> *Thirty days hath September,*
> *April, June and November.*
> *All the rest have thirty one,*
> *Except February alone.*
> *That has twenty — eight days,*
> *Twenty — nine in a leap year.*

● What day of the week was the last day of September 1991?

This calendar uses two cubes to display the date. Each date uses both cubes. The 1st is displayed as 01, the 2nd as 02 and so on.

● What numbers go on each cube?

Glossary

counting numbers 1, 2, 3, 4, 5 and so on. The whole positive numbers.

difference what remains when you subtract one number from another

even numbers numbers which can be exactly divided by two, with no remainder

index another word for "power." The plural is indices.

power the power of a number tells you how many times to multiply the number by itself. 5^3 means 5 to the power 3 or $5 \times 5 \times 5$ which is 125.

prime numbers numbers which cannot be divided exactly by any other number except 1. 2, 3, 5 and 7 are prime numbers; 4 is not because 4 can be divided exactly by 2.

micron a very small unit of measurement. It is one millionth of a meter.

multiple the multiples of 3 are 3, 6, 9, 12, 15 and so on. They are the numbers which divide exactly by 3 with no remainder. They are the 3 times table, continued as far as you like. The multiples of a number are all the numbers which can be divided exactly by that number.

scientific notation a way of writing very large and very small numbers without using lots of digits. It uses the powers/ indices of 10.

Answers

62

Page 7 See page 8 for answers to dots.
The code is A = 2, B = 4, C = 6 and so on.
Michael Jackson magic number 248
Charlie Chaplin magic number 238
Winston Churchill magic number 416
George Bush magic number 214
Queen Elizabeth magic number 300
Madonna magic number 124

Page 8 See page 11 for dot arrangements.
4th odd number $= 7 = (4 \times 2) - 1$
5th odd number $= 9 = (5 \times 2) - 1$
50th odd number $= 99 = (50 \times 2) - 1$

Page 10

7	8	3
2	6	10
9	4	5

1.

11	4	9
6	8	10
7	12	5

2.

24	3	18
9	15	21
12	27	6

3.

20	6	16
10	14	18
12	22	8

4.

7	2	3
0	4	8
5	6	1

5.

10	5	6
3	7	11
8	9	4

6.

8	3	10
9	7	5
4	11	6

7.

4	9	8
11	7	3
6	5	10

8.

6	11	4
5	7	9
10	3	8

9.

The last four squares are the same numbers in the same order but rotated through 90 degrees each time.
The magic number in Emporer Yu's square is 15.
The total of all the numbers is 45.

Page 11 See page 14.

Page 13

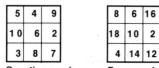

5	4	9
10	6	2
3	8	7

8	6	16
18	10	2
4	14	12

Counting numbers   **Even numbers**

1. One way of knowing whether a group of numbers will make a magic square is to arrange them in ascending order. If the sum of each pair of numbers on either side of the middle number is twice the middle number, then the numbers will form a magic square.

7	12	1	14
2	13	8	11
16	3	10	5
9	6	15	4

1.

16	2	3	13
5	11	10	8
9	7	6	12
4	14	15	1

2.

13	8	12	1
3	10	6	15
2	11	7	14
16	5	9	4

3.

21	7	8	18
10	16	15	13
14	12	11	17
9	19	20	6

4.

Page 14 24 had the most patterns. The square numbers were: 9, 16 and 49   For the answer to the investigation, see page 16.

Page 16 The next three square numbers are: 36, 49, 64.
The sum of the first fifteen odd numbers is 225 (15^2)
$18^2 = 17^2 + $ 18th odd number $= 289 + 35 = 324$

Page 17 7th triangle number $= 28$

Page 18 10th triangular number $= \frac{1}{2}$ of the 10th square number $+ 5 = 55$

Page 20 1. Multiply by 3, subtract 1
2. Square the number (Multiply it by itself)
3. Add 1, divide by 2 **4.** Multiply by 5, add 2

Page 22 5. 3, 6, 9, 12, 15, 18, 21, 24, 27
6. 2, 4, 6, 8, 10, 12, 14, 16, 18
7. 5, 7, 8, 19, $\frac{1}{5}$, 1, 16, 40, 3

Page 26 $10 = 10^1$ $1 = 10^0$ $13,000 = 1.3 \times 10^4$
710 million $= 7.1 \times 10^8$ $0.00004 = 4 \times 10^{-5}$
$0.000781 = 7.81 \times 10^{-4}$ a centrillion $= 1 \times 10^{600}$

Page 28 Grains on 20th square $= 2^{19} = 524,288$

Number of square	Number of grains on square	Sum of grains	Pattern
4	$2^3 = 8$	15	$2^4 - 1$
5	$2^4 = 16$	31	$2^5 - 1$
6	$2^5 = 32$	63	$2^6 - 1$
64	$2^{63} = 9.2234 \times 10^{18}$	1.8447×10^{19}	$2^{64} - 1$

Your answer will depend on what sort of rice you weigh and how accurately you weigh and count it. Using rice at 200 grains to $\frac{1}{8}$ oz., it would take 800 million trucks!

Page 29
The next three numbers are 34, 55 and 89.

Page 30
1. The Fibonacci sequence appears again.
2. The difference is always 1.
3. The difference is always 1 again, whichever group you choose.
4. Yes, it always happens.
5. As the numbers in the sequence get bigger the answer settles down to 1.618.

Page 31
They are a pair of Fibonacci numbers. 1.618 was called the Golden Ratio by the Greeks. They thought that buildings, with dimensions in that proportion, were the most pleasing.

Page 32 101 dots will give the 100th triangle number which is $\frac{1}{2}$ of $100^2 + 50 = 5,050$
The pattern in the number of lines is the sequence of triangular numbers. 3 dots gives the 2nd triangular number, 4 dots the 3rd triangular number and so on.

Page 33 Number Chains
1. The chain always ends up 4-2-1-2-1 and so on.
2. The chain still ends up 4-2-1-2-1 and so on.
3. The chain sometimes breaks down into fractions.

Elevenses

The pattern seems to build up with an increasing number of numbers, the same as the power of 11, between two 11's.

The 6 in 1 4 6 4 1 suggests that the pattern may not continue.

Page 34 Move 4 The player chooses 2 to block the opponent's winning move next time.

Move 5 Choose 7 to block the opponent.

Page 37 Numbers around a triangle The smallest number possible is 9 – the sum of the biggest number and the two smallest numbers. The greatest total possible is 12 – the sum of the smallest number and the two greatest numbers. 10 and 11 have also been found. Other solutions will be reflections or rotations of these four solutions.

```
        1                    1                    6                    6
        ●                    ●                    ●                    ●
   5 ●    ● 6          4 ●    ● 6          3 ●    ● 1          2 ●    ● 1
   ●   ●   ●           ●   ●   ●           ●   ●   ●           ●   ●   ●
   3   4   2           5   2   3           2   5   4           4   3   5

      Total 9            Total 10             Total 11             Total 12
```

Numbers from 1 to 10 These are some ways of making the numbers from 1 to 10, you may find others that work.

1 $(3 \div 1) - (4 \div 2)$ **2** $4 + 2 - 3 - 1$ **3** $2 + 4 - (1 \times 3)$
4 $4 + 1 + 2 - 3$ **5** $(4 \times 1 \div 2) + 3$ **6** $4 + 3 + 1 - 2$
7 $1 + (3 \times 4 \div 2)$ **8** $2 + 3 + 4 - 1$ **9** $(2 \times 3) + (4 - 1)$
10 $1 + 2 + 3 + 4$ or $(2 \times 3) + (4 \times 1)$

Star number The solution is to put 4 in the middle and a pair of numbers which total 8 on the ends of each line.

Page 38 See page 40.

Page 39 See page 40.

Page 40 1. 5 coins can fall $2^5 = 32$ ways.

2. 4 coins and 5 exits both produce the pattern 1 4 6 4 1.

Page 43 The counting numbers are in the second and next to last diagonal rows.

The fifth row of the triangle is the same pattern as the way 4 coins can fall.

The sixth row gives the pattern for five coins.

The triangular numbers are in the third and second to last diagonal rows.

The tenth row will total $2^9 = 512$.

Page 44 1. All the odd numbers have been shaded. They form three triangles, each with an even number in the center.

2. The multiples of 5 have been shaded. They form a triangle.

3. The multiples of 3 have been shaded. They form three triangles.

4. The multiples of 7 have been shaded. They form a straight line. If you carry on the triangle, the multiples of 7 form another triangle.

Page 45 They are the numbers of the Fibonacci sequence. The number in the square is the sum of the numbers in the diagonal.

The numbers in the squares are the triangular numbers. The sum of $1 + 2 + 3 + 4 + 5 + 6 + 7 + 8 + 9 = 45$

Page 46

Number of times folded	Number of sections	Number creases
1	2 (2^1)	1
2	4 (2^2)	3 ($2^2 - 1$)
3	8 (2^3)	7 ($2^3 - 1$)
4	16 (2^4)	15 ($2^4 - 1$)
5	32	31
10	1024 (2^{10})	1023 ($2^8 - 1$)

Page 47

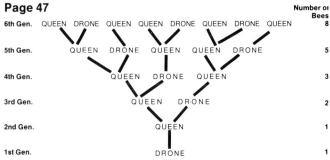

There would be 13 bees in the seventh generation.
It is the Fibonacci sequence

Page 48 1. The multiples of 3 have been shaded.
A no B no C yes D yes
2. The multiples of 4 have been shaded.
A yes B no C no D yes
3. The multiples of 6 and the multiples of 7 have been shaded. A no B no C no D yes

Page 49 4. A = 49 (7^2) B = 65 ($8^2 + 1$) 100 will be in the top right hand corner square.
5. A = 96 ($2 \times 7^2 - 2$)
B = 72 (2×6^2)
C = 200

Page 50 1. A = 60   B = 86   C = 118
2. A = 36   B = 608   C = 1,408
3. A = 595   B = 798   C = 991

Page 51 Multiples of 5 have been shaded.

Page 55 See pages 56-57

Page 57 See page 58

Page 58 10 frogs will take 15 moves; 9 frogs will take 14 moves.

Page 59 The Saturdays go up in sevens because the calendar is arranged in a pattern of weeks.

Page 60 The 29th was the last Monday of July. The 24th was a Wednesday. The last day of September 1991 was a Monday.

Cube 1 0, 1, 2, 3, 4, 5

Cube 2 0, 1, 2, 6, 7, 8 (6 can be turned upside down for 9)

Index